THE WACKY WORLD OF THE
3 STOOGES

THE WACKY WORLD OF THE 3 STOOGES

Annie McGarry

BISON GROUP

First published in 1992 by
Bison Books Ltd
Kimbolton House
117 A Fulham Rd
London SW3 6RL

ISBN 0 86124 978 X

Printed in Hong Kong

Designed by Tom Debolski

Previous pages: *Moe is on the other end of the abuse in* Idiots Deluxe *(1945).*
At right: *Larry, Moe and Curly learn that what goes up must come down.*

CONTENTS

INTRODUCTION

What's the Big Idea?

Ask any American anywhere, from nursery schools to nursing homes, about the Three Stooges, and they'll undoubtedly know the eye-poking, pie-throwing trio: Moe, the stern, black-browed taskmaster; Larry, the fidgeting fence-sitter; and Curly, the dunce of dunces, a bull in a china store with the grace of a ballerina. Then there's Shemp, and Joe and Curly Joe. (The Stooges were three in name only.) They heckled one another, served as the butts of their own jokes and honed a fine edge on the broadest slapstick around. In fact, the Stooges were used to define 'Comedy' in the *World Book Encyclopedia*. Pictured below the comedy heading and the only photograph on the page are Larry and Moe, wrapping a crowbar around Curly's neck. Veterans all of minstrel shows and vaudeville, they brought their act to motion pictures for a 35-year film career, introducing every generation to the wonders of 'Nyuk, nyuk, nyuk, woo, woo, woo, woo.'

Moe, Larry, Curly and the others got their figurative eye-pokes from disparaging theatre owners, crooked comedy partners, and studios who took advantage of their naivete. But as millions of Stoogeophiles know, this comedy team could take whatever frying-pan-over-the-head the world had to offer and still be ready for the pie-in-the-face. Their career together was spotted with contractual difficulties, personnel changes, imposed retirements and lapses in popularity, but the Stooges persevered. They took their knocks, pulled their punches, and in their final years enjoyed a revival unrivalled by that of any other comedy team.

Moe Howard was a Stooge first and last, as well as the first and last Stooge. Moe was Ted Healy's first stooge, back in 1922 before they were even officially called 'Stooges.' Moe remained a Stooge throughout, except for a brief and unsuccessful venture into the workaday world in 1927 while Shemp and Ted Healy were doing Broadway. Later, when the decision was made to leave Healy, Moe became the leader of the act. Throughout the many personnel changes of the team, Moe remained, becoming famous for barking out commands and threats such as 'Spread out!' 'Break it up!' 'I'll murder ya!' and 'Why, I oughta… .' As long as there was still Stooging to be done, Moe was eager to do it.

Shemp Howard, the second to join up with Ted Healy and his little brother Moe, enjoyed a 'split shift' with the Stooges beginning in 1925.

Previous page: *The Stooges look down upon their suave alter egos. Curly seems shocked by Jerome Howard, Larry winces at Larry Fine, and Moe glowers at Harry Moses Howard.*
Below: *The boys provide some harmony in* Disorder in the Court.
Facing page: *Larry has some bad luck walking under ladders.*

Shemp and Ted spent 1927 on Broadway while Moe was assailing the business world. After the first breakup with Healy, Shemp spent another three years with Larry and Moe, and then departed to pursue his successful solo career as Knobby Walsh in the Joe Palooka shorts. He also appeared in many other movies, including some with Abbott and Costello and some from the Dagwood and Blondie series. But once a Stooge.... After Curly's death fifteen years later, Shemp rejoined the Stooges until his own death in 1957.

Larry also joined up in 1925, and was a Stooge for the next 40 years, from the first short until the last feature. Larry is a quiet but crucial Stooge, balancing and buffering Moe's surliness and Curly's silliness. Larry is the calm in the storm.

Curly replaced his brother Shemp in 1932, just as the Stooges' film career was beginning. Curly, the clear favorite of most Stooges fans, made 97 Stooge shorts before his stroke in 1945, when Shemp rotated back in to cover for Curly. Curly made his last appearance as a Stooge in 1947, in a cameo which joined the three Howard brothers on film for the first and only time.

Finding another Stooge after Shemp's death was not easy. There were no more Howard brothers in show business, waiting in the wings. Joe Besser joined on for 15 shorts in 1957 and 1958, and Curly-Joe DeRita replaced *him* for 10 features made between 1959 and 1965, as well as innumerable personal appearances.

Many have tried to explain their mystique. Steve Allen calls them the 'masters of... bumping-into-each-other, falling-down, pie-in-the-face comedy.' Jack Kerouac stated that the Stooges had 'worked out every refinement of bopping each other.' Critic Brooks Atkinson expressed it rather eloquently when he described Shemp, Larry and Moe as 'three of the frowziest numskulls ever assembled.' But there is more to their special charm than superb slapstick. Children and adults fancy seeing three grown men cavorting about like unruly boys. It makes kids feel smarter than adults, and adults feel as though they can remain child-like forever.

Under the Stooge name, these stars of slapstick appeared in over 194 shorts and five feature-length films, and made countless personal appearances. On Broadway and in films, they co-starred with the likes of Al Jolson, Jimmy Durante, Clark Gable, and Laurel and Hardy, and appeared in **Dancing Lady**, starring Joan Crawford and Fred Astaire. **Men in Black**, their spoof on the wildly popular Clark Gable film, **Men in White**, garnered an Academy Award nomination, while the original got no recognition from the Academy at all.

Almost three decades after they made their last film, Stooges fan clubs continue to flourish, the film festivals sell out, and their comic genius is televised worldwide. The family of Stooges devotees gains new converts daily. Among the old enthusiasts: Steve Allen, Michael Jackson, Jack Kerouac...the list goes on. And the show goes on, as every old vaudevillian knows it must.

STOOGE ROOTS

Fugitive Lovers

Solomon and Jennie Gorovitz were the progenitors of Stoogedom, parenting three out of the four men that we remember most often when we think of the Stooges: Shemp, Moe and Curly Howard, and Larry Fine. In Czarist Russia, Sol and Jennie were married young and sent off to America in order to evade Sol's impending military conscription and the anti-Semitism of the Russian army. In 1890, they arrived at Castle Garden, New York, where Jennie's thick Lithuanian accent caused the immigration official to record the family name as 'Horwitz.' And so it remained, for Jennie and Sol, anyway. The next generation—Moe, Curly and Shemp—would later change the name again, to Howard.

Sol and Jennie had two sons, Irving and Jack, soon after they had settled in Brooklyn. Their third son, and the first-born of the men who would be Stooges, was Samuel, who came into the world on 17 March 1895. Again, Jennie's heavy accent altered a family name: 'Sam' came out sounding like 'Shemps.' The Horwitz boys and their neighborhood friends preferred that odd name to 'Samuel,' and the nickname stayed with him for the rest of his life.

Baby Sitters' Jitters

Shemp, a mischievous and gregarious kid, began 'rehearsing' for his life as a Stooge early. At age six, Shemp sneaked away from the very first Horwitz family picnic, loaded with the tomatoes he had stolen from little Moe's plate. He was dragged back moments later, kicking and screaming, by a man dripping head to toe with said tomatoes. The man began to shake Shemp, which infuriated Jennie. She began beating the man with her sun umbrella, and soon everyone had joined in the fray. When the air finally cleared, Sol had a bloody nose, Jennie was still swinging her umbrella (which was later determined to have given Sol his bloody nose), Moe had been pelted by crockery, and Shemp was screaming like a banshee, though no one had touched him. Yet.

Since Shemp was more a class clown and hooky aficionado than a scholar, Jennie spent as much (or more) time down at the school as he did. The day of Shemp's graduation from grade school, when Shemp approached the stage for his diploma, the principal said, 'Ladies and gentlemen, this young man did not graduate—his mother did.'

Previous page: *The Stooges find their way to Egypt to locate a valuable mummy named Rootin' Tootin' Kamen in* We Want Our Mummy *(1938).*
Below: *Curly may get smacked in his smock in* Pop Goes the Easel *(1935).*
Facing page: *Moe watches someone else lose his temper in* Movie Maniacs *(1936).*

Moe, born Harry Moses Horwitz on 19 June 1897, rivalled his brother in truancy and other mischief. He fought his way through school, when he was there. One spring he attended school only 40 days out of a possible 103. In his words, 'Sometimes I fought about my curls, sometimes I just raised hell.' Later known for his stick-straight black bowl cut, as a child Moe had long banana curls that Jennie twisted into his hair each morning. Jennie seemed to derive such pleasure from these curls that little 'Harry' hadn't the heart to tell her that they were the bane of his existence, the cause of the bruises and black eyes that weren't really gotten while playing. He simply prayed that the next baby would be a girl with long curls, for Jennie's sake and his own.

The next baby, much to Moe's disappointment, was not only the fifth Horwitz boy, but also had straight hair. Ironically, years later, upon shaving his head he dubbed himself Curly. Jerome Lester Horwitz's first pet name, however, was 'Babe,' given to him by his brothers. Born 22 October 1903, Babe was the first Stooges stunt man, always placed in precarious positions by Shemp and Moe.

One afternoon, babysitters Moe and Shemp converted Babe's brand-new baby carriage into a soapbox racer, and were ready to let their brother give it a down-hill test-drive when Sol and Jennie arrived home in time to save their son. That scolding didn't stop Moe, however, from testing his dead-shot aim in games of William Tell with his baby brother. From the very beginning, Curly was a victim of 'soicumstances.'

Turn Back the Clock

In the 1890s, a young Fannie Lieberman went with her friends to see a gypsy fortune teller at the edge of town. The woman pulled her aside and told her, 'You will marry, and have a son who will be known all over the world.'

Meanwhile, in Russia, young Joseph Frienchicov wanted out of the Russian army. Like Solomon Gorovitz, Joseph was plagued by the anti-Semitism of his officers and fellow soldiers. He had unknowingly beaten out his sergeant's cousin for a spot playing horn in the Czar's Army Band, and the sergeant was trying to sabotage him. Joseph eventually fled to England and then to America, where his brother lived as Nathan Feinberg. There he met Fannie, and true to the gypsy's word, they married and had a son who…. But that's getting ahead of the story.

Their first son, Louis, was born on 5 October 1902, in the tiny bedroom above Joseph's jewelry store. Known as 'Larry,' he was a born performer. At age two he would entertain customers at his father's shop with impromptu tap dances on display cases. As if in preparation for his future career, he once crashed through a glass-topped case while doing so, and emerged unhurt from the scattered brooches and rings.

On a darker note, at age four, Larry spilled some oxalic acid on his arm, and only surgery and skin grafts saved it from amputation. As therapy, the doctor recommended violin playing. Little Larry took to the cure, and soon he was first violinist at Southwark Grammar School. His teachers and parents had hopes of his becoming a concert violinist, but ragtime interceded. A friend put some Scott Joplin on the Feinberg's Gramophone, and soon a 13-year-old Larry was sneaking off to buy sheet music and converting his orchestra friends to the new sound.

HI DIDDLE DEE DEE, AN ACTOR'S LIFE FOR ME

Loco Boy Makes Good

Back in Bensonhurst, Moe Horwitz decided at the age of 11 to become an actor. He started going to the theatre more often than he went to school. To finance his tickets and carfare, he sold frogs in saloons (15 cents apiece, or 10 for a dollar), but the greatest portion of his earnings went to help support his family. There is no record of what Moe's patrons actually *did* with the frogs.

Once in their teens, Moe and Shemp began putting on shows for their friends, usually using little Curly for the female leads. Seven-year-old Curly had trouble remembering his lines, a problem which he never quite outgrew. Years later, it was this same difficulty that spurred him on to improvisational greatness. As early as 1910, Moe—already the established leader of the family theatre troupe—eventually solved the problem by writing Curly some cue cards—on adhesive tape across Moe's own forehead.

Not content to perform only in living rooms and backyards, Moe got himself into motion pictures. In 1909, he took the train down to the Brooklyn Vitagraph Studio and offered his services as a go-fer for the actors, free of charge. His refusal of tips aroused curiousity and garnered him the attention he wanted, and he was soon put to work in small roles. Moe's acting career had to remain a secret, though. In order to become a thespian, he was playing hooky from school.

The summer of 1912 found Moe and his best friend, Lee Nash, performing as members of the Annette Kellerman Diving Girls, diving thirty feet into a pool seven feet long, seven feet wide and seven feet deep. The troupe was comprised of six girls and four boys pretending to be girls. The boys filled out their one-piece women's suits with newspaper, which they had to rearrange underwater after every dive.

Shemp matured into a fine Chaplinesque clown. He played the ukulele extremely well, and was quick with a joke or a wild story. He and Moe, who played the straight man, began entertaining their friends at parties, and their success convinced them to try professional vaude-

**Previous page: Moe Howard gives the look that probably could kill in this studio still.
Above: Larry Fine looks anxious as usual.
Facing page, top left: Curly is not quite clear on the concept of fishing in Whoops, I'm an Indian (1936).
Facing page, top right: Curly's got a dame on each arm in Ants in the Pantry (1936).
Christine McIntyre doesn't seem alarmed as (facing page, bottom) the Stooges play firefighters who fight over her in False Alarms (1936).**

ville. Shemp had just gotten a blackface act written, however, when Moe landed himself a job on a Mississippi showboat with Captain Billy Bryant, a famous impresario.

The Captain Hates the Sea, or Commotion on the Ocean

Moe had answered an ad in Billboard magazine asking for a young man of average height with his own wardrobe. He was only 5'4", and had no clothes to speak of, but he did have a great deal of determination and nerve. Moe sent a photograph of a neighbor who was a model, passing the handsome boy off as himself. He didn't mention his height or his age. When Shemp learned of his would-be partner's deceit, he warned him that he'd end up breaking rocks on a chain gang. Then he lent him $10 and wished him luck.

Captain Bryant had sent Moe a very expensive train ticket to Jackson, Mississippi, where the *Sunflower* was docked, and was outraged to discover Moe's cozenage. He assigned Moe some janitorial tasks and garnished his wages to cover the train fare and the new ad which would be run for his replacement. By the second week, however, Moe had cajoled an audition, which he won. Moe was overjoyed, able at last to do what he loved best—act. By the end of his second and final season with the Captain, his salary had risen from $20 a week to $100. He was ready to finally go home, and join his brother Shemp in the glorious tradition of vaudeville.

Everyone has to start somewhere. In the case of Howard and Howard (which they used as their stage names, thinking that that sounded better than Horwitz and Horwitz), they debuted professionally as the 'clean-up' act at the Mystic Theater on 53rd Street near Third Avenue. When the theater would fill up, the manager would send in the clowns, Moe and Shemp, and their corny jokes would promptly drive out the audience to make room for the new ticket-buyers lined up outside. The humiliation didn't faze the boys too much, and they saw their material, timing and presence improve. The salary, unfortunately, remained the same—next to nothing.

The Yoke's On Me, or Half-Wits' Holiday

By 1916, Sol and Jennie Horwitz had bought a farm in Chatham, New York. They were new to farming, and didn't know much about it. For example, shortly after buying the farm, Jennie sold an enormous pig to the neighbors because it was not kosher. Two weeks later, the pig had a large (and valuable) litter of piglets.

Moe and Shemp knew even less about farming, but during the summer, they left the sticky heat of New York City to go north to 'help out.' While they were down on the farm, they had a certain costume they liked to wear: red flannel Union suits, Continental Army coats and tricornered, Early American military hats. Shemp tended the cows in this garb. When a neighbor would drive by in his horse and buggy, Shemp would strike and hold a fantastic pose in the middle of the field. Neighbors often stopped by the Horwitz farm to remark upon their strange scarecrow.

Jennie wired the boys at the farm that she was coming for the weekend, and would they please pick her up at the train station. In preparation for their mother's arrival, Shemp shaved off only the left

Below: *Larry and Curly take orders from Moe in Gripes, Grunts and Groans (1937). Facing page: Larry, Moe and Curly make a habit out of hunting in Ants in the Pantry (1936), but their hostess seems horrified by their quarry.*

side of his big, bushy beard, while Moe shaved off only the right side of his. They donned their favorite costumes and drove off to the station in a surrey with a fringe on top.

When their mother arrived, she stood looking around the station for several minutes without actually recognizing her two sons, who were standing stiffly by the surrey, each holding a horse by the bridle. Jennie finally heard Curly's giggles coming from behind these two motley madmen, and as she went to find him, Moe and Shemp each took her by an arm and kissed her on each cheek. By then, a small crowd had gathered, and the staid Jennie Horwitz was mortified. She asked her sons, 'How can you do such crazy things? The people will think you're *meshugana!*'

During the summers and at planting and harvest times, Moe and Shemp helped their brother Jack tend the farm. The rest of the year, by defying a disapproving Jennie, they were free to develop their vaudevillian talents.

A Victim of Soicumstances, or Flat Foot Stooges

As Moe and Shemp pursued their theatrical careers, Curly watched his big brothers with great admiration and vowed to join them some day in show business. In the meantime, he was eager to learn from Moe

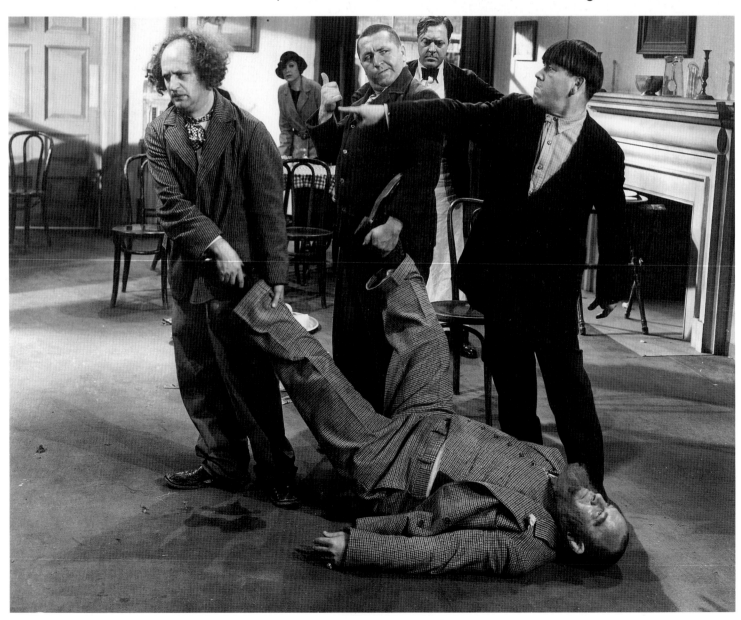

how to do the work on the farm: separating the cream, churning the butter and feeding the livestock at 4:30 am. Curly spent the rest of his time dancing, going to the beach and playing his ukulele. And although Curly was a great animal lover, he also loved to hunt.

That summer, when Curly was 13 years old, he went hunting with a neighbor. He took along his prized possession, a .22 caliber rifle, which had a hair trigger. At one point, Curly was resting with the gun in his lap, fiddling absent-mindedly with the trigger, and the gun discharged into his ankle. Moe and the other boys rushed him to the hospital in Albany, over 60 miles away, where he remained for a week. No one knew at first whether or not Curly would lose his foot.

When at last that danger seemed past, the doctor recommended that Curly have the bones in his instep and his ankle broken in six months and reset. Curly panicked, having never been in the hospital before, and immediately vetoed the doctor's advice. Curly had a life-long limp as a result of that decision, but he used it in his comedy, and he never let it interfere with his dancing.

All the World's A Stooge

The Loew's and RKO vaudeville circuits had an agreement never to use the same performers simultaneously. In 1917, at the ages of 20 and 22, Moe and Shemp were covertly working on both circuits. The Howards bypassed this rule by performing under different names—in blackface for RKO and in whiteface for Loew's.

In 1922, Moe and Shemp saw an ad announcing that Ted and Betty

Healy were appearing at Brooklyn's Prospect Theater. Ted Healy was the stage name taken by the former diving 'girl,' and Moe's boyhood best friend, Lee Nash. They decided to go in and heckle their old pal. Despite 10 years' separation, Ted immediately recognized the obnoxious pair in the front row, and brought them up on stage as volunteers. Ted had the trapezes lowered and told Moe and Shemp to hop on. He gave the stage hands a signal, and up went Moe and Shemp to the rafters, where they stayed for the rest of the show. Shemp, who was terrified of heights, carried on like a banshee, but only between acts.

Healy had some auditions with booking agents coming up, and asked Moe to help him out for a couple days. Those two days turned into nine years. The routine they worked up was so successful that before long they were touring the South, making $3500 a week. The split: Ted got $3400, and Moe received $100.

STOOGE: *n* 1. an entertainer who feeds lines to the main comedian and usually serves as the butt of his jokes 2. originally, in the theater, a paid heckler who harassed the comedian on the stage from a seat in the audience **3. one who allows himself to be used for another's profit**

The year 1925 was full of major changes for all the Stooges. Both Moe and Shemp were married, Moe to Helen Schonberger, a cousin of Harry Houdini, and Shemp to Gertrude 'Babe' Frank, the daughter of a builder from Bensonhurst. The year also marked the beginnings of a new comedy phenomenon: the Stooges.

Moe and Ted were working at the Orpheum in Brooklyn, when Moe heard an unmistakable laugh come from the audience. He whispered to Ted that Shemp was somewhere out there. Ted asked for a volunteer from the audience, preferably someone, he said, from Brooklyn. Shemp sauntered up to the stage munching on a pear, which he then offered to Ted. Ted refused, Shemp tried to force it on him, Ted smashed the pear into Shemp's face, and a new trio for tumult was born. In that same year a fourth prankster joined the pack: the Howards finally crossed paths with Larry Fine.

Vernon Dent, an actor frequently seen in the Stooges' movies, usually played the much put upon innocent bystander outraged by the Stooges' antics. In Half-Shot Shooters (1936), Dent tries to enjoy his chicken despite four pairs of hungry eyes (facing page); later, he makes a convincing army recruitment officer (above).
Overleaf: *The boys perform dubious service for their country as they prepare to shell their target, which is actually the admiral's ship.*

STOOGE: *n* 1. an entertainer who feeds lines to the main comedian and usually serves as the butt of his jokes **2. originally, in the theater, a paid heckler who harassed the comedian on the stage from a seat in the audience** 3. one who allows himself to be used for another's profit

Above: *Doctors Fine, Howard and Howard bring the fountain of youth to their patient in* Dizzy Doctors *(1937).*
Facing page, top: *Vernon Dent's expression could peel paint when he sees the wax job the Stooges gave his car in* Dizzy Doctors *(1937).*
Facing page, below: *The Stooges and their wives attempt to build their own home in* The Sitter-Downers *(1938).*

Fiddlers Three, or Fling in the Ring

Meanwhile, young Louie Feinberg (better known as Larry Fine) was also making inroads on the world of entertainment, via amateur nights. Larry was small for a 13-year-old, about 4'2", and he dressed himself up in a Buster Brown outfit, making himself seem seven or eight years old. He played ragtime violin and sang. Everyone thought he was a prodigy. Ironically, Larry would be wearing virtually the same outfit as a full-grown man in **Hello Pop** 18 years later.

It was 1915, and vaudeville was just starting to 'give the hook' to the minstrel show as the most popular entertainment venue. Emmett Welsh, a minstrel impresario, was looking to develop a new act: project the words of a song on a movie screen so the audience could sing along. Mr Welsh's idea was to use these 'commercials' as an added feature at the newest type of theatre, the movie house, which would eventually give the hook to vaudeville. The songs got plugged, and more sheet music got sold. It was Larry's first break: he marched up and down the aisles, playing the violin and rousing everyone to sing along.

Larry entered and won a lot of Charlie Chaplin look-alike contests, and even had a brief career as a professional lightweight boxer. Fiddling had helped Larry's arm recover from the acid burn, and the doctor wanted Larry to engage in some more strenuous therapy, so Larry chose boxing. Much to his parents' dismay, he became quite good at it. Larry fought and won his one and only pro match under the alias 'Kid Roth.' Despite his subterfuge, his parents found out, and his father appeared at the end of the match to drag a victorious Larry out

of the ring by his ear. As Larry's brother Morris said, 'When he and Dad left, no one could say Larry was retiring undefeated.'

GI Wanna Go Home

In 1916, Larry had gone off to New York to join the cast of **The Newsboy Sextet**, but homesickness and a cold drove him home for some chicken soup. Still only 14, he felt his career had failed, that he wasn't even worthy of an amateur night. He decided to give up show business, and worked briefly as a rivet passer on an assembly line in Philadelphia, building ships for the First World War. He would later use his experience on this assembly line in a riveting scene in a 1940 Stooges movie, **How High Is Up?**

Being in the factory cheered Larry up, and he began playing amateur nights again, dancing the *kazotchka* in the Russian-Jewish style while playing **My Old Kentucky Home** on his violin. He was a one-man melting pot. With his backside just inches above the floor, his feet flew out in front of him like a defective windmill. Larry kept his tall silk hat from flying off, and didn't step on his own silk tails.

Larry quit passing rivets, and began working with friends on an act called the Keystone Komedy Kwartette, named in honor of Mack Sennett's great comedy shorts studio. Meanwhile, Larry's father, Joseph, believing that Larry should have *real* work, started him in the family jewelry business. With Larry behind the counter doing *shtick*, however, the fine jewelry store turned into a de facto vaudeville theatre. After less than two months, Joseph was convinced that Larry was meant to be on stage. In acknowledgment of show business' victory, his father gave Larry two week's salary and a bonus of $100 to stay away from the business world forever. Larry kept his side of the bargain. At age 15, he got a job as a violinist with Howard Lanin's Orchestra, and he never again worked as anything but an entertainer.

The war had created a whole new venue for performers: military bases full of restless and nervous young soldiers. Larry began working the circuit with a partner, Nancy Decker, until a young dancer named Mabel Haney convinced Nancy to join the Haney Sisters. Without Nancy, Larry very quickly went through a series of female partners. One such partner's name was Winona Fine. They couldn't bring themselves to call the act Fine and Fine, so they went by Fine and Dandy. Unfortunately, they weren't. No one seemed to work out.

Larry tried to break in a single act, usually working the 'blackout,' while the stagehands were changing sets. He met Jules Black, who was putting together **School Days**, an act not unlike **The Newsboy Sextet** with whom Larry had performed in New York. Shows based on classrooms were incredibly popular, but what really persuaded Larry to join was his chance to work with Mabel Haney, the same young dancer who had stolen Larry's best partner. He didn't hold a grudge, though: after the act finished a five-year run, Larry and Mabel were married.

Larry wrote an act and went on the road with Mabel and her sister Loretta. They wound up in Chicago, at the Rainbo Room and Jai Alai Fronton, a casino and night club. He happened to be playing cards with Fred Mann and the other producers when the old emcee quit. Suddenly, Larry found himself with a seven year contract as emcee. Here, the story becomes confusing: Moe, always quick to cop the credit, claimed that he discovered Larry in 1925, while other sources hold that Shemp was responsible for finding Larry in 1928.

**Facing page, above: *With pickax and map, Moe tries to get rich quick by going on a treasure hunt in* Cash and Carry *(1937).*
Facing page, below: *Prospecting Stooges strike it rich when they unknowingly tunnel into Fort Knox.*
Above: *Moe, Larry and the watchman (played by Dudley Dickerson) mistake a plaster-covered Curly for a ghost in* A Gem of a Jam *(1943).*

MERRY MAVERICKS

From *Three Missing Links* to *Start Cheering*

According to Moe, he and Ted Healy caught Larry's *kazotchka*-with-fiddle act at the Rainbo Gardens in 1925. He asked Ted, 'Are you thinking what I'm thinking?' and Ted replied, 'Yes, I'm thinking what you're thinking!' They went backstage, where Larry has just gotten out of the shower. His hair was drying in its wild way which was later to become his signature. Ted offered him $90 a week—$10 more if he'd drop the violin. Larry accepted.

There was only one problem: Larry's seven-year contract with Fred Mann at the Rainbo Room. Fate stepped in when, just a few days later, the Rainbo Room was closed down for violating Prohibition laws. Ted, Larry, Shemp and Moe became Ted Healy and His Three Southern Gentlemen.

The other version of the story holds that in 1928, Shemp was working in Al Jolson's **A Night in Spain**, but wanted out so he could go do another act, and was trying desperately to find his own replacement. Al Jolson and the rest of the cast of were being honored at the Rainbo Room, and Larry was the roast master, doing his Jolson imitation for Jolson himself. Shemp was extolling Larry's comedic virtuosity, trying to persuade Ted to make Larry a Healyite. Ted protested that Larry looked so young and innocent that people would call Ted a child beater when he cuffed him on stage.

Shemp was Ted's favorite stooge, and he didn't want to let him go. He liked the weather-beaten quality of Shemp's face. He thought Shemp looked dumb and dangerous, like an escaped convict. But, as Shemp insisted, Larry *was* the right size for a stooge—standing 5'4"—and a few evenings spent 'looking for Aunt Mathilda' would cure Larry of his cherubic appearance. (On Ted Healy's infamous bar-hopping safaris, he traditionally pronounced that no one could go home until they had met his Aunt Mathilda.)

Finally, Healy was persuaded by Larry's improvisational talent—as well as Shemp's threats to leave Ted high and dry—and called him over. 'Hey, kid, do you want to be in **A Night in Spain**?' Healy asked.

'Why? Jolson's not good enough for you?' Larry bantered.

He was certain that Healy was kidding with him. When he realized that Healy was serious, Larry hesitated. He would come watch the show

Previous page: *By the time he appeared in* **A Pain in the Pullman** *in 1936, Larry Fine had had much professional experience hanging around with monkeys.*
Above: *Larry got to play his violin in several shorts, including* **Termites of 1938** *(1938).*
Facing page: *The Stooges perform with cowgirls in a saloon chorus line in* **Goofs and Saddles** *(1937).*

before he decided whether or not to break his contract at the Rainbo Room. An exasperated Healy intimated that Larry might prefer Broadway with Al Jolson to roasting celebrities in a casino. He then suggested that Larry get a better feel for the show by watching from the wings.

STOOGE: *n* **1. an entertainer who feeds lines to the main comedian and usually serves as the butt of his jokes** 2. originally, in the theater, a paid heckler who harassed the comedian on the stage from a seat in the audience 3. one who allows himself to be used for another's profit

Standing in the wings, Larry was somewhat dazed and bewildered by the commotion of the show, as well as the quick turn of events that had so radically changed his life that day. In one afternoon, he had gone from gambling away his earnings as a 'glorified maitre d' (as Ted referred to him) to being offered a spot on Broadway with the greatest star alive.

At a certain point as Larry watched the show that night, Jolson himself was standing right behind him. At a signal from Healy, Larry got a hard shove from Jolson and found himself out in front of a capacity crowd. He was at the mercy of Healy and had no idea of what would happen next.

The audience must have thought that Larry was doing a great impression of a very frightened man. Healy abused a cowering Larry mer-

cilessly for a few minutes. Occassionally he'd feed Larry a line under his breath, which would only set Larry up to be a bigger fool. Finally, Larry escaped off-stage. Healy found him, and asked him what he wanted to do for the next act. Larry thought about telling Healy what *he* could do for the next act. Realizing he was in the hands of a madman, however, he decided to just climb aboard the roller coaster.

I Can Hardly Wait

Meanwhile, Curly was at odd ends. He didn't work. Even though he was in his mid-20s, his mother supported him. He was the only bachelor left of the five brothers. He wanted to go into show business, but his mother disapproved. She had already 'lost' two of her sons to that cursed vaudeville, and she didn't want to lose her baby. Curly saw very little of Moe and Shemp during the early twenties when they were travelling the vaudeville circuit, but Moe in particular wrote a lot of letters to little 'Babe.'

Curly was secretly wed in 1928, but even members of the family do not know the name of the mysterious woman who was Curly's first wife. They had been married for several months when Curly was forced to reveal his clandestine wedlock. He had discovered that two couldn't live as cheaply as one, and went to his mother for a loan. Jennie was furious that her youngest son had gotten married. She would support *him* but not his wife. Curly, determined never to take money from his

Above: *The boys modestly cover their faces with veils as John Lester Johnson (in white turban) and Vernon Dent (far right) inspect the new 'harem girls' in* Wee Wee Monsieur *(1938).*
Facing page: *Eddie Laughton plays the Bronx cab driver who takes a fare to Egypt in* We Want Our Mummy *(1938).*

mother again, went out and got his first job in show business. He was 25 years old.

Despite her disapproval of his becoming an entertainer, Curly was anxious for his mother to see the show. Reluctantly, she agreed. In a black swallow-tail coat, he stood in front of the Orville Knapp Orchestra, his exaggerated tails sweeping the floor, gracefully waving his baton, as his 'cutaway' coat did just that—slowly ripping apart until Curly was left conducting the band in long underwear, his pants around his ankles, with a giant safety pin holding up the drop-seat. Curly's mother was shocked. This burlesque was no job for Jennie's son. Two weeks later, she had convinced Curly to divorce his new wife and quit his job with Orville Knapp's band.

Meanwhile, Moe and Shemp were getting back into vaudeville, this time as Ted Healy and the Racketeers, and Jennie didn't want Curly anywhere in the vicinity. Jennie decided to take Curly and Sol on a European vacation. The purpose of this diversion was to get her son's mind off his two lost loves: show business and his wife. However, she *did* allow Curly to stay in Paris alone while she went to her hometown in Lithuania.

Curly reveled in the Parisian night life, and away from his mother, he became more his own man—as well as a bit of a *ladies'* man. When he returned to Brooklyn in 1929, he resumed his conducting duties with Orville Knapp despite Jennie's protests.

Malice in the Palace

Life in show business wasn't quite as glamorous as Curly imagined. Ted Healy and the Racketeers performed, or tried to, at a party of the Black & White Society (so named because the men wear black dress shirts, white tie and dinner jackets; the women wear white evening dresses with black scarves).

The evening was supposed to be very elegant and posh, so the boys rented tuxedos and a piano player. When they arrived, however, all the guests were drunk. Shemp, Moe, Larry and Ted were trailed constantly by the woman who had hired them, who was afraid that they were going to make a *faux pas*. When Larry tried to talk to some of the women, she whispered in his ear, 'You performers are not to mingle with the guests.' When Larry obediently turned to go, one of these delicate flowers of society vomited on him. Larry rented a busboy's jacket for five dollars to replace his own ruined rented tuxedo, and they went on stage. Immediately, audience members began to pelt them with dinner rolls. Ted Healy shouted, 'Let's hold out for the roast beef!'

However, when the fracas gained gale force, they ran for their lives. The crazy world of vaudeville was nothing compared to some of the '*high* society' parties, and both venues provided the boys with inspiration for many movie plots.

Monkey Businessmen

In 1927, while Shemp and Ted went off to do **A Night in Spain**, Moe and his wife had their first child. Moe decided to leave show business and live a respectable life, so he became a building contractor. The image of Moe on site, knocking hard hats together and snarling, 'Spread out' is a funny one, but this career didn't last too long. Moe was short on business sense, and soon had to file for bankruptcy.

Now almost penniless, he gave the business world one more try: he invested his last dollars in 'distressed merchandise' and opened a junk store. His biggest success was selling mesh bloomers. He missed the theater, though, and when he and Helen, his wife, sold the store just five weeks later, he never looked back.

That night, in desperation, Moe called up Ted Healy, who had a proposition: would Moe, Shemp and Larry like to appear with him in **A Night in Spain** on Broadway? Helen told Moe to say that he would sleep on it and call him in the morning, but there was no sleep for Moe that night. He called Ted back in the middle of the night, unable to wait any longer to get back into the business. The next morning, Ted's chauffeur picked up Moe and his family and brought them out to his 26-room home in Darien, Connecticut.

All during his performing life, no matter what kind of dive he was playing, Larry would always exclaim, 'Next stop, the Palace!' Every

Facing page: Caveman Larry tussels with the gorilla head while Curly stands revealed in the suit, and a cavewoman begs caveman Moe for mercy in Three Missing Links (1938).
Below: 'Washer-woman' Curly pops out of a laundry basket with the missing baby, as dog-washers-turned-kidnappers-turned-laundrymen Larry and Moe look on with the police, the parents and their dalmatian, in Mutts to You (1938).

Above: *You can dress these boys up, but you can't take them out. Silverware becomes peashooters in a game of William Tell as a horrified society matron looks on.*
Facing page, above: *This pony isn't sure what to make of the tales being whispered in his ear by Curly, Moe and Larry.*
Facing page, below: *The Stooges ply their trade as tinkers. Moe and Larry take a tongue-lashing while Curly takes notes.*

vaudevillian's dream was to play the legendary New York theater, and Ted Healy and his Racketeers got their chance. The team consisted of Ted, Larry, Moe, Shemp and Fred Sanborn, a xylophonist. The *New York Times* referred to the act as 'rough and hardy sport, but unendingly funny.' One patron reported that the ushers were running up and down the aisles serving water to the audience, who were laughing so hard, they were choking. A Twentieth Century-Fox studio representative who was there that night saw the bedlam, and brought Ted Healy and his Racketeers to Hollywood.

STOOGE: *n* 1. an entertainer who feeds lines to the main comedian and usually serves as the butt of his jokes 2. originally, in the theater, a paid heckler who harassed the comedian on the stage from a seat in the audience **3. one who allows himself to be used for another's profit**

Gypped in the Penthouse

The boys made their collective film debut in the 1930 film **Soup to Nuts**, written by Rube Goldberg, the popular cartoonist and inventor. Ted received $1250 a week, of which each stooge received their customary $100. After the film was completed, Winnie Sheehan, the head of Fox Studios at the time, offered Moe, Shemp and Larry (but not Ted) a seven-year contract. Several days later, someone from Fox called and said that the deal was off. The boys didn't know what to

Below: *They may look innocent when they are asleep, but Edna Oliver isn't fooled in* Rocking Through the Rockies *(1940).* **Facing page:** *Moe, Eddie Laughton and Larry can read the writing on the wall, or on Curly's undershirt if need be.*

make of the news. Soon afterward, Moe was told by someone that Ted had gone to Sheehan and said, 'You know, Mr Sheehan, you're ruining my act by signing the boys. I didn't think one Irishman would do this to another.' Sheehan told him not to worry, he would take care of it, and dropped the boys from Fox.

With their Fox contract cancelled, Moe, Larry and Shemp had planned to go back to Healy, but word of this betrayal changed everything. They decided to proceed without Healy, as Howard, Fine and Howard—Three Lost Souls. 'Who's afraid of the big, bad Healy?' Larry used to ask. Eventually, they would find out how fearsome their former leader could be.

During nervous rehearsals of their new act, the new trio tried to relax over games of three-handed bridge. One day when Larry wasn't playing well, Shemp became incensed, leaned over and invented the infamous two-fingered eye-poke (don't try this at home, kids.) Moe laughed so hard that he literally fell off his chair; he went through a glass door, still laughing. Larry was crying, and Shemp was apologising profusely. Larry couldn't see the humor in it, couldn't, in fact, see much of anything at the moment, but Moe, his arm cut by the glass and bleeding, thought it was the funniest thing he'd ever seen.

The poke was incorporated into the act the next day, Moe assuring Larry that he would practice 'the Sign of the Stooge' only on Shemp. 'Dead Shot' Moe, in all the years he used this gag, never once hit anyone square in the eye.

Goof on the Roof

Another characteristic Stooge move was also taken from real-life pranks. The Three Lost Souls were appearing in a vaudeville house in Kansas City. The day was sunny, and Moe was bored, so he decided to go up to the roof to sunbathe, leaving the rest of the fellows sitting by the stage door. As he passed the open dressing room door of a dance troupe, he noticed an uneaten piece of blueberry pie on a tray of dirty dishes. Moe said later, 'The scene just kind of triggered something.' He asked the girls if he could have the pie, went up to the roof and peeked over the edge, where he could see Larry's head shining down below. Moe lined up the pie with the target, and let it fall. It was a perfect hit.

After impact, Larry looked up and heard laughter coming from the open window of the dancers' dressing room. He stormed up, saw the remaining pie pieces on the tray, and made the obvious and erroneous connection. Larry wiped some pie from his brow, stuffed it into one man's mouth, smeared pie all over his suit, and all over the dressing room walls. The dressing room erupted into screams and curses, and Larry walked outside, only to bump into Moe. 'Okay, Dead Shot,' Larry said. 'How come the blue on your hand matches the blue on my head?'

Whenever there was a pie to be thrown, Moe was the one to throw it, unless it was being thrown at him. Later, during their film career at Columbia Pictures, one producer figured that Moe had probably saved the studio thousands of dollars in time and film, not to mention cream puffs and pies, with his William Tell accuracy.

Above: *From their early days with Ted Healy comes this old movie poster for the 1934 musical comedy extravaganza,* **The Big Idea.** *The Stooges were known at the time as* **His (Healy's) Three Stooges,** *with their last names in parentheses.* **Facing page:** *Curly demonstrates his talent with the spoons as an annoyed Joan Crawford glares. Larry's hair is still mild-mannered in this 1934 MGM musical.*

Uncivil Warriors, or Disorder in the Court

As the Three Lost Souls were gaining a name for themselves, Ted Healy and three other stooges were set to open at the Roxy Theatre in New York. After the first performance, the manager told him to walk out on the show, because the new stooges were going to ruin him. They had no sense of timing and didn't understand the act. Healy took his advice, but couldn't find replacements. He tried to break up Howard, Fine and Howard by luring Larry away, but Larry remained loyal to the Howard brothers.

Meanwhile, the Three Lost Souls hired a new straight man named Jack Walsh, and had begun performing at New York's Hippodrome Theater. Healy was not ready to let bygones be bygones. He threatened the Hippodrome with a lawsuit if Howard, Fine and Howard used 'his' material. If anyone, the material belonged to JJ Shubert, who produced **A Night in Spain** and **A Night in Venice**. Shubert took the boys' side. He had a pretty good idea of Healy's character because he had himself been involved in lawsuits with Healy. Healy then sent three thugs to threaten the stooges with bodily harm if they didn't stop performing. In a scenario which smacks of a good Stooges' plot, they didn't fulfill their mission. Instead, they were converted to 'Stoogeophiles' as they watched Howard, Fine and Howard's act.

Eventually, Healy admitted he needed them and begged them to come back. Moe and Larry went to Healy's hotel room, but Shemp refused to go. Meanwhile, Healy's drinking problem had reached a new low. He was suffering from DTs and missing performances. He begged Moe and Larry to work with him again, and Moe finally agreed, on the condition that Ted stop drinking. However, Shemp was understandably reluctant to get mixed up again with the man who had cheated them and caused them so much trouble. Although they had been friends since they were young, Shemp knew that Ted's actions were unpredictable. He had to say no.

Shemp went on to appear as Knobby Walsh in a long series of Joe Palooka movies. It would not be for 15 years, after a successful independent career, that he would get another crack at Stoogehood.

Whoops I'm an Indian

When Shemp left the troop in 1932, Moe sent for their baby brother, who was still conducting for Orville Knapp, and still going by his real name, Jerome Horwitz. 'Jerome' tried to do his comic conductor bit for Healy, and Healy laughed him off the stage. His response was, 'Is that all he can do? Get me a real comedian!'

At the same time, Healy had delivered an even more withering insult when he said Jerome looked too 'normal.' The Man Who Would Be Stooge went home, rehearsed Shemp's parts with Larry and Moe, and shaved off his beautiful, wavy hair. When he returned the next day, Healy didn't even recognize him, and hired him. When Healy asked for his name, he christened himself with his reply: 'Curly. Curly Howard.'

In the early days, Ted wouldn't let Curly do much of anything. He was not 'allowed' to do Shemp's material; mostly he just skipped across the stage dressed in a tight-fitting bathing suit, splashing a little pail of water. Curly looked like a monstrous baby, a big, bald Humpty Dumpty. He got some laughs, but he knew he could get more. Little by little, he began incorporating bits of Shemp's material (as well as some

of his own) back into the act. Healy couldn't object because the audience loved it.

In 1933, Ted Healy & His Stooges were booked into the Club New Yorker in the Christie Hotel in Hollywood. There was only one problem—how to get there. Ted had enough money to pay either his hotel bill or the train fare for six people to California. Ted owed the people at the Park Crescent $1200, and all of his belongings were still in his room. Hotels tend to be somewhat sensitive when vaudevillians leave the premises with unpaid bills and a lot of trunks and suitcases, so the boys devised a scheme. With cabs waiting out front, each of them went up to the room with a friend, and layered as much of Ted's clothing as they could over their own. Considering that the average stooge was about 5'4" and Ted was 6'2", they must have been quite a sight making their getaway. When the elevator doors opened, they did a shuffle-off-to-Buffalo through the lobby, followed by Curly doing a cute little dance as the clerk waved good-bye.

The boys and their wives celebrated their shot at stardom on a festive cross-country train ride, then arrived in Hollywood just days before the notorious Long Beach earthquake. On 10 May 1933, as the house was shaking violently, Moe found Curly pounding on Ted's door, yelling at him to stop whatever he was doing. He was convinced that the shuddering of the house was just another of Ted's pranks.

HOLLYWOOD PARTY

Out West

Clark Gable, Carole Lombard, Spencer Tracy, Jean Harlow and Buster Keaton were among the full house at the Stooges' opening night at the New Yorker Cafe in March 1933, and soon after, MGM signed them for a one-year contract—with Ted Healy.

During 1933, Healy's Stooges made five two-reelers for MGM that combined slapstick comedy and musical dance numbers. They went on to make four or five features for the studio, co-starring the likes of Jimmy Durante, Clark Gable, and Laurel and Hardy. They made an appearance in **Dancing Lady**, starring Joan Crawford and Fred Astaire. Other studios, such as Paramount, Columbia and Universal, began to clamor for their services.

Ted made a half dozen or so films without the Stooges, which made Moe suspicious—maybe Ted was interested in a strictly solo career, thereby saving himself the $100 a week he was paying each of them. The boys were strolling the MGM lot one day in May of 1934 when they ran into Ted and his agent. Moe simply said that Ted didn't need them anymore, and that they should just part amicably. Ted looked at his agent, who agreed with Moe, and then ran off to get releases.

Studio Stoops

Once the split was official, the boys sat down on a bench at the MGM lot to decide on their new name. Since they had always been Ted Healy's stooges, they decided to call themselves the Three Stooges. On his way to his car a few minutes later, Moe ran into an agent named Walter Kane, who asked Moe to accompany him to Columbia Studios. He felt sure he could get them a contract. Moe met with studio head Harry Cohn that afternoon and signed a temporary paper.

Meanwhile, Larry was about to leave the MGM lot when he ran into Joe Rivkin, another agent, who invited him to Universal Studios. There, Larry signed a form contract, stamped with the date and time.

Later that day, when they congregated at Moe's apartment, Moe announced his good news—and then Larry announced *his* good news. Two rights made a big wrong. For the next 37 years of his life, Larry didn't do any more business for the act. When Moe told Harry Cohn

Previous page: Clark Gable visits with Ted Healy and His Three Stooges on the set of Danc- ing Lady. The ensemble resembles nothing so much as Prince Charming surrounded by four of the Seven Dwarfs. Above: Moe and Larry try to pass Curly off as an undis- covered opera singer. When the phonograph Curly has been secretly lip-synching along with is unplugged, he feigns laryn- gitis (facing page).

what had happened, he laughed and said, 'You know, Moe, this story would make a hell of a movie!' He then called both legal departments, checked the times stamped on the contracts, and found out Columbia had beaten Universal to the punch, or, more accurately, to the punchers.

Larry, Curly and Moe made their first two-reel comedy for Colum- bia, **Women Haters**, in 1934. A musical all in rhyme, the Stooges appeared in the film separately, not as a team. Larry starred, and Moe and Curly were featured in supporting roles. After **Women Haters**, Columbia decided to sign the Three Stooges to a long-term deal: a seven-year contract with yearly options requiring eight two-reel come- dies in a 40-week period with a 12-week layoff to do whatever they wished—except make films elsewhere. Their salary was $7500 a film, making a yearly total of $60,000.

The Stooges were thrilled with the deal, not realizing the ramifica- tions of some of the fine print. One clause stated that Columbia had the right to use their voices and likenesses as well as any film product in any medium existing then or *to be invented*. In 1958, when Columbia's subsidiary Screen Gems released the 194 Stooge shorts, they quickly became standards of syndicated television, but the Stooges received no royalties. The Stooges lost out financially again when the Screen Actors' Guild, under the leadership of then-president Ronald Reagan, instituted a ruling that there would be no residuals for films made prior to 1960.

The Tooth Will Out

The Stooges suffered some physical abuse, as well, in pursuit of top-notch slapstick: bloody noses, cuts from flying glass and many, many bruises. In *Three Little Pigskins* (1934), the boys take the role of football players, while the other 'actors' were actual Loyola University football players who outweighed Larry, Curly and Moe by at least 50 pounds each. In one scene, the entire team was supposed to pile up on top of the Three Stooges. They may have been Stooges, but they weren't stupid. The boys demanded stunt doubles against the director's protests about cost and time considerations. An hour later, two of the doubles had broken legs, and the four actors on the sidelines all had either broken arms or legs. The only one who didn't have to go to the hospital was Curly's double, who was thickly padded to resemble the corpulent Stooge.

In *Ants in the Pantry* (1936), the Stooges play exterminators who are having trouble drumming up work. Under threats from their boss, A Mouser, they covertly *give* bugs to people, so that they can then exterminate them. They sneak into a mansion where a fox-hunting party is taking place, and put moths in with the minks, mice in the kitchen, and ants in the pantry. During filming, a container of red ants broke apart in Moe's pocket, and ants began crawling all over him. He was scratching, squirming and slapping himself all over, including the seat of his

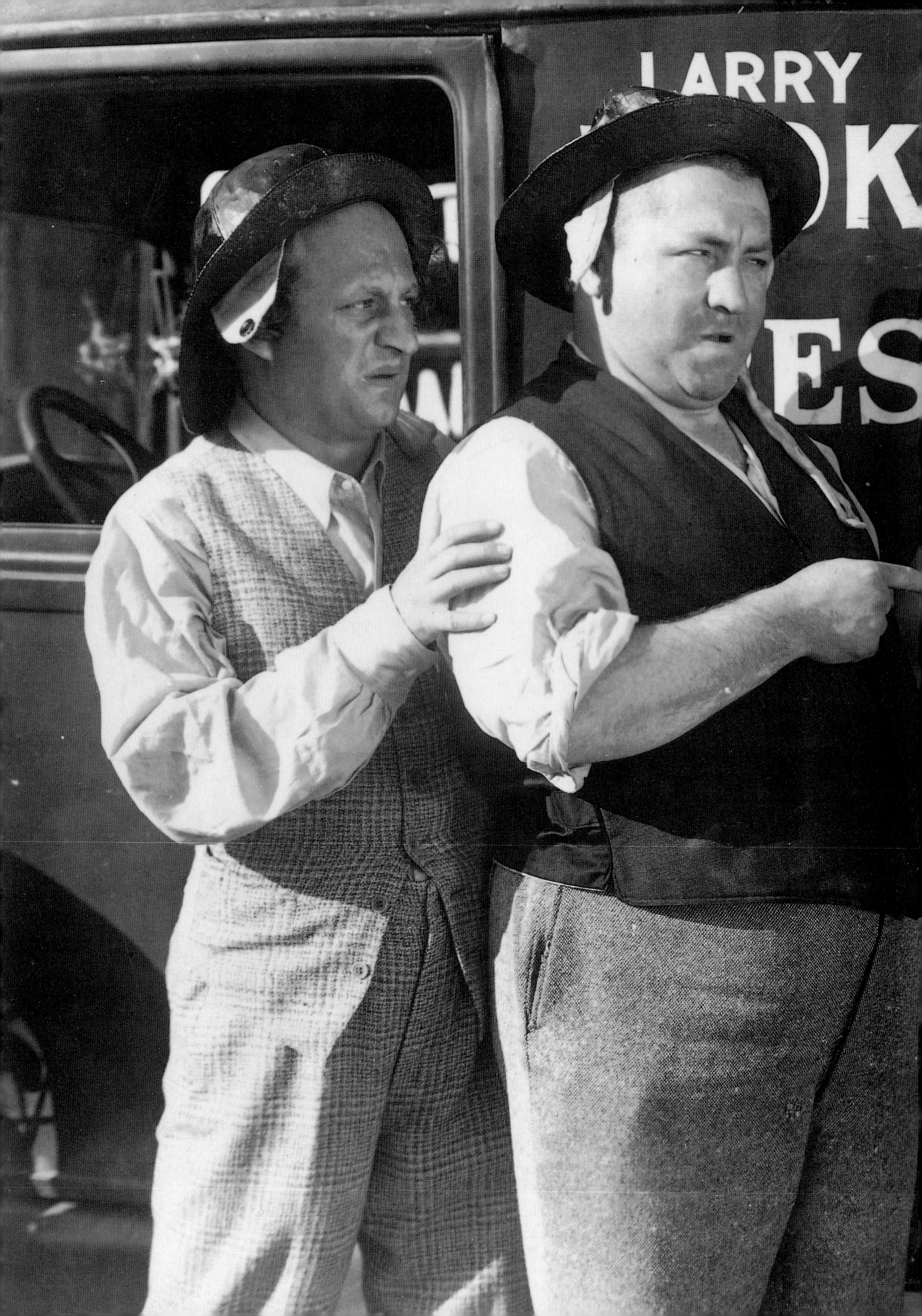
LARRY

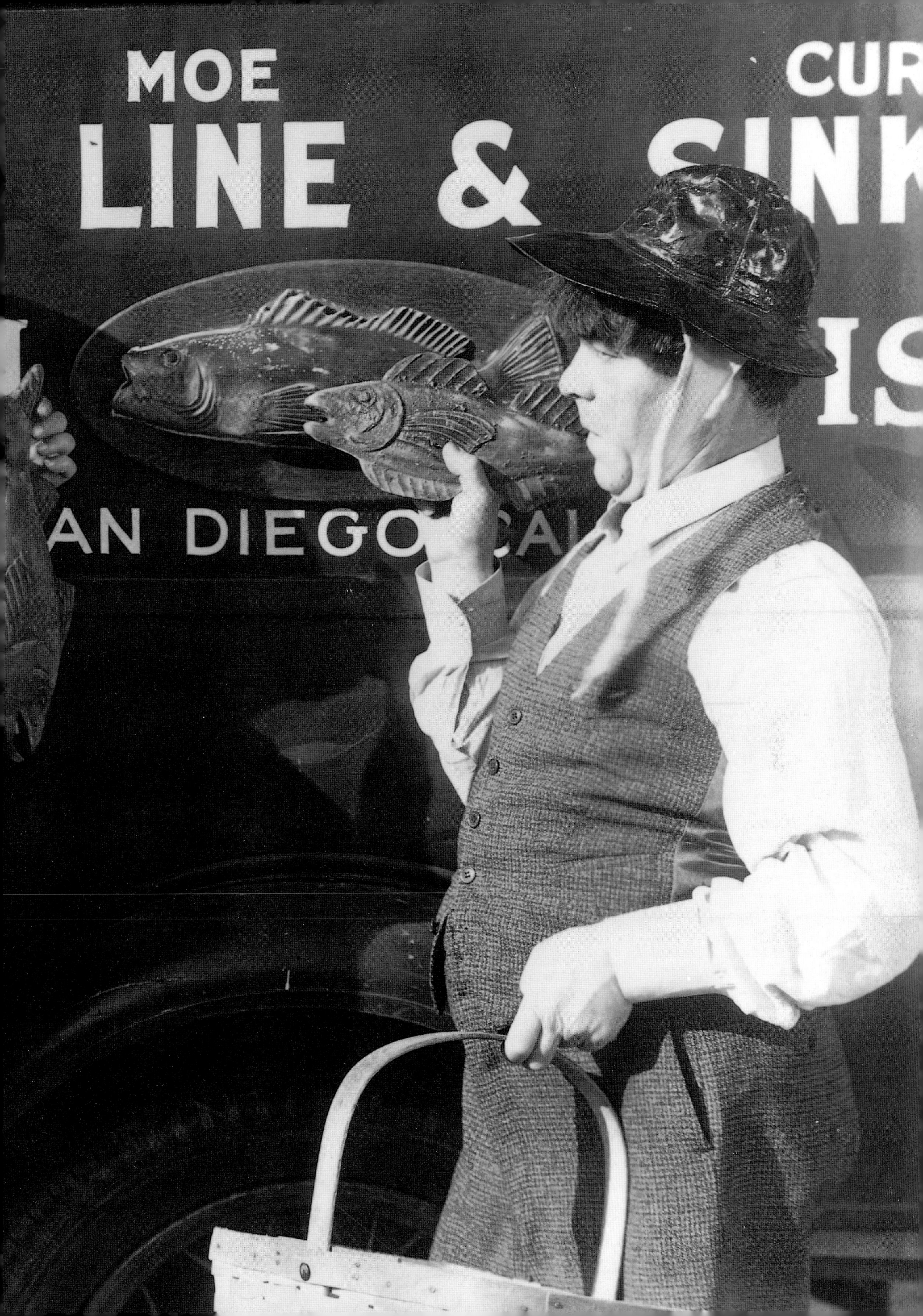
MOE
CUR
LINE & SINK
AN DIEGO

48

Previous pages: *Larry Hook, Moe Line and Curly Sinker, San Diego fish salesmen, talk fish.*
Above: *The Stooges are tinkers, not thinkers.*
Facing page, above: *The Stooges open a beauty parlor south of the border in* Loco Boy Makes Good *with Bob O'Connor.*
Facing page, below: *Curly reveals the true identity of the villain.*

pants. Everyone thought the scene was hilarious. Everyone except Moe, of course.

In one short, Curly was supposed to fall down an elevator shaft. The special effects man constructed a hole in the stage and covered the bottom of the hole with a mattress, but neglected to cover the sides. Curly went in, hit his head on the two-by-fours, and cut his scalp open. The studio doctor washed the cut and sealed it with colodion. The makeup man covered the wound, and Curly, a bit wobbly, went on with the show.

Once, when Curly went to the doctor for an ear infection, the doctor removed a cherry pit from his ear. It must have gotten stuck during a pie fight.

The fans could be hazardous as well. Children and drunks, especially, doled out as much punishment as Moe, only they didn't pull their punches. Believing Curly's head to be as indestructible as it seemed in the movies, strangers would often come up and smack him on it. Once in Atlantic City, a little boy ran up and cracked a cane over Curly's head. Curly turned, fists clenched, dazed but furious, and saw this little boy, with his mother beaming right behind him. Curly took a small Curly-style bow before his legs buckled.

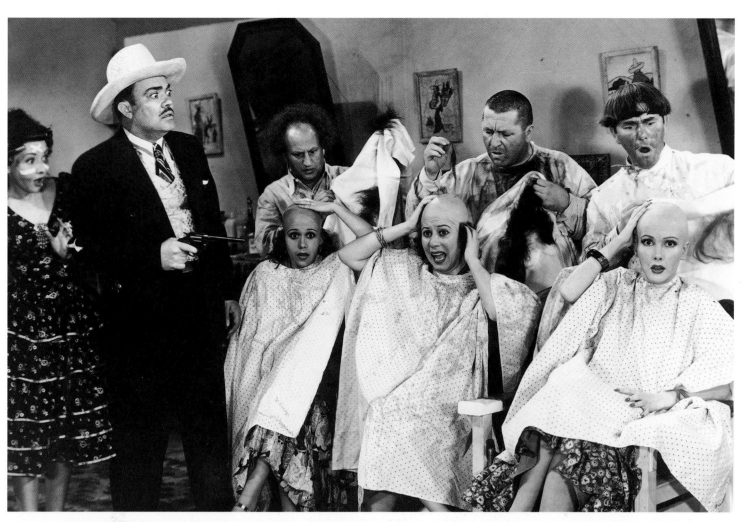

THE SHORTS END OF THE SHTICK

Pies and Guys

The movies which inspired such mania are well-known to just about everyone who has attended an American grade school or seen a television. Who among us can say that they've never attempted (or privately tried to perfect) the Curlyesque finger-snapping-fist-slapping routine, accompanied perhaps by a 'nyuk, nyuk, nyuk'?

Among the few uninitiated, and with those who have not enjoyed the trio since puberty's onset, the Stooges have a reputation for doing little more than knocking each other around, throwing pies and poking eyes. Considering the artistry of their slapstick, that would certainly be enough for fine comedy. But the Stooges' humor is much more. Clever word-play and satire is as prevalent as gushing seltzer bottles.

In **Ants in the Pantry** (1936), a particular favorite among many fans, Curly tries to pass himself off at a posh party as a college-educated man. With his usual killer instinct for people putting on airs, Moe asks him, 'Oh, yeah? What school'd you go to?' Curly, acting very proud and distinguished, replies 'Oxford.' Moe grimaces, kicks him in the ankle, and says, 'Well, you better go back to high shoes.'

One might impress a disdainful highbrow by likening the Stooges to Shakespeare's clowns. Like the buffoons in **Midsummer Night's Dream**, **Romeo and Juliet**, and **Twelfth Night**, the Stooges have finessed the art of the insult. They say to each other what we could never say to our siblings, at least not while Mom or Dad were around. When Larry gleefully exclaims, 'We're filthy with dough!' Moe tells him, 'You're filthy without it.'

When Curly's sweetheart dotes upon her pet, a monkey named Darwin, he innocently asks, 'What's that monkey got that I haven't got?' Moe replies, 'A longer tail.'

In **Spook Louder** (1943), Curly Q Link (the Q stands for Quff, of course), the long-sought heir to his uncle Robert's (Bob O Link) fortune, shows up for the reading of the will. 'You must be the missing Link!' exclaims the butler — another evolution joke.

The sort of sophisticates who might not appreciate the Stooges *oeuvre* were often direct targets of their playful satire. At a time when many Americans were suffering the financial blows of the Great

Depression, the Stooges' films were peopled by wealthy snobs with phony British accents, butlers, poodles and affected manners. These monied megalomaniacs and matrons do little else than chat at cocktail parties about gossip, lion hunts and riding to the hounds. The Stooges could always be counted on to push a few pies into their turned-up noses, and to make a mansion with a minor plumbing problem resemble a fire hydrant capped by a sieve.

Curly was never daunted by the aristocracy. In **A-Plumbing We Will Go** (1940), Moe instructs Curly, 'We're society, so we got to act like society.' Curly replies, 'I ain't gonna act *that* dopey.' When Larry tries to parrot society talk at a fancy party in **Ants in the Pantry** (1936), Curly doesn't play along:

Larry: Whatever happened in 1776?

Curly: What street?

When the manager of the Costa Plente Hotel brags that their bed goes back to Henry the VIII, Curly informs him, 'That's nothing. We had a bed go back to Sears Roebuck the third.'

Curly knows how to make a grand exit out of a mansion. In **Calling All Curs** (1939), the Great Bald One belly-flops onto a liquor cart, yelling 'Mush!' to the hapless mutt who has the considerable job of hauling Curly.

The Stooges are definitely down-and-outers, but always *just* on the brink of winning on a horse or a radio contest, or coming into a huge inheritance. When Moe pulls a horse-shoe out of the soup Curly has served him, he glowers, 'We sent ya to the *butcher shop* for meat, not the glue factory!'

But even when times are hard, Curly won't compromise on his standards for his employment. Moe reads an ad from the Help Wanted section of the paper: 'Wanted: Waiter. Free uniforms, free transportation, free lunches, free sleep quarters and *free cigarettes*!'

Larry exclaims, 'Oh, boy, free cigarettes!'

Curly, however, is not so easily impressed: 'What? No matches? I wouldn't work for that piker!'

The boys have their share of trouble with the law, with many vague references made to time spent in the Big House. Upon entering almost any house, Larry will remark that it reminds him of the reformatory. When an Irish policeman tells Curly, who is dressed as a woman, that 'she' reminds him of a colleen in County Cork, Curly replies, 'Oh. You remind me of a cop in county jail.' When asked if he were familiar with the Great Wall of China, Curly answers, 'No, but I know a big fence in Chicago.' Whether caught nicking a watermelon off a horse-drawn cart, or taking a punch at a policeman Curly *thought* was a statue, the

Stooges can always evade the coppers by sneaking into a magician's disappearing act, or dressing up as 'dames.'

The boys had their share of gallows humor. One time, the feckless fellows are framed for a murder and sent to Death Row. A radio announcer intones into a microphone, 'Howdy, folks, howdy, this is your old friend Bill Stein, bringing you a jerk-by-jerk description of the triple hanging of the Mushroom Murder Mob. This broadcast is coming to you from Hang-'em-All Prison. We're at the gallows-side, and it's a beautiful day for a hanging.'

In the stands, a vendor is hawking his wares to eager cons in striped suits and hats: 'Peanuts! Popcorn! Sody pop! Candy! Get yer pro-grams, *all* the names and numbers, ya can't tell the victims apart without a program. Program?' Just as they're about to swing, the boys are found innocent, pardoned and cut down. That's not to say that the Stooges were ever *entirely* innocent. They enjoy their vices. Confront an on-screen Stooge with a choice between a stogie, a betty, and an inside tip on a long-shot horse (typically one so sway-backed that it resembles a hammock), and he wouldn't know what to do. Poker is a favorite pastime among the Stooges. As Larry says when Curly is working on a radio jingle, 'Why dontcha play cards and improve your mind?'

In **Ants in the Pantry** (1936), their boss's secretary reports that Larry, Curly and Moe are in the office discussing politics. The boss finds this hard to believe. The secretary substantiates her claim with a vigorous

The Three Stooges in some of their many confrontations with the authorities.
Facing page, above: A police-man stands between a housewife and soldiers Larry, Moe and Curly in GI Wanna Go Home (1946).
Facing page, below: Vernon Dent (second from the left) always got his Stooges—though usually not for long.
Above: The boys are jailed for bootlegging in Beer Barrel Pole-cats (1946).

The military was another one of the Stooges' favorite subjects, especially during the World War II years.

Above: Sailors Moe, Curly and Larry offer raspberries and other unconventional forms of salute to officer Vernon Dent in Back From the Front (1943).

At left: Larry, Curly and Moe seek military advice from a fortune teller in You Nazty Spy (1940).

In I'll Never Heil Again (1941): Moe, Larry and Curly meet a fraulein (facing page, above); and Duncan Renaldo (far left), Larry, Moe, Curly and others dive for the globe in the parody of World War II (facing page, below).

58

Below: *Curly got some wall-paper stuck on him, but he trusts Larry and Moe to lend a helping hand—or in this case, a hot iron and a blow torch.*
Facing page: *Curly makes a new friend in* **Phony Express** *(1943).*

nod of her head: 'Yes! I just heard one of them say, "Let's have a New Deal!"' The camera cuts, of course, to Larry shuffling a deck of cards under a cloud of cigar smoke.

In that same game, when Larry's four aces beat Moe's four kings, Moe discovers dozens of aces under Larry's seat. After an eye-poke and a whack, Moe recites his moral code: 'If you want to cheat, cheat fair.'

In the 1938 short, **Mutts to You**, Larry, Curly and Moe play professional dogwashers who inadvertently kidnap a rich client's little boy. The film may well have served as the inspiration for **Three Men and a Baby** (1987)—the three grown men dote and coo over the cherubic baby, and are completely inept at baby maintenance such as diapering and burping.

Soup to Nuts (1930), the first Stooge film to be released, was written by Rube Goldberg, the cartoonist and inventor. Rube was best known for his wildly extravagant machines created to perform simple tasks, like a mouse-trap with the size and mechanical complexity of a car. Rube's influence is definitely felt in **Mutts to You** (1938). The dog-washing machine involves flying bird cages, a conveyor belt, a chute, rubbery hands suspended from the ceiling, an enormous flea-killer, and Curly in foul weather gear riding a stationary bicycle. The shingle hung outside the shack pulls no punches:

**'DOGS WASHED WHILE YOU WATE. 50¢
MOE. CURLY. LARRY. PROPS'**

The Stooges didn't even need the props. Their shorts had earned them millions of loyal fans who simply loved to watch them stumble in and out of scrapes. The fans' affection for these rascals had made them rich, famous, major Hollywood stars. But what really seemed to impress Larry, Curly and Moe was the devotion of their fans.

Curly

In 1945, Curly's health began to fail. Years of carousing, smoking Havana cigars and drinking had taken a toll on his health. On the set of his 97th short, **Half-Wit's Holiday** (1947), a remake of **Hoi Polloi** (1935), Moe went over to see why Curly hadn't responded to the assistant director's call. Moe found Curly with his head on his chest, unable to speak, crying silently. Soon, both men were crying. Curly had suffered his first stroke. Moe sent Curly home, but had to finish a final scene for the day before he could join him there.

Curly's stroke was severe, but left him only partially paralyzed. With no money coming in, high medical expenses and his taste for the finer things in life, Curly was having financial problems. In the movies, Curly had always overcome seemingly insurmountable odds with a bark or some fancy footwork, but now he desperately needed the help and support of his fellow Stooges. Moe and Shemp, without being asked,

Overleaf: Moe sends the blades spinning as Larry looks distinctly nervous and Curly just hangs on in Dizzy Pilots (1943).

began giving a percentage of their weekly paychecks to Curly. Larry, while not a Howard brother but still *mishpocheh*, or one of the family, also insisted upon contributing an equal share.

In 1947, Moe, encouraged by Curly's signs of improvement, made arrangements for Curly to make a cameo appearance in **Hold That Lion** (1947). With a thick head of hair, a derby hat and a clothespin on his nose, the super Stooge was still impossible to miss. It was the only time all four of the major Stooges were in one film together. Curly never made a full recovery, however, and after suffering several more strokes, he died at the age of 49.

Curly had a broad influence on comedy. When Abbott & Costello were performing in a minstrel show in Atlantic City, they watched the Stooges at every opportunity from the wings of the Steel Pier. Moe always felt that there was much of Curly in Lou Costello's mannerisms and high-pitched voice. Others have traced Curly influences in John Belushi's comedic persona—the little boy in the overgrown body, sometimes petulant, throwing a tantrum, or else sweet and coy. Donald O'Connor admitted that he stole a dance move from Curly—the Curly spin-on-the-floor in **Singin' in the Rain** (1952). It was this same move that inspired the break-dancers in the '80s to perform the Coffee Grinder, sometimes to the tune of the Curly Shuffle.

Facing page, above: Curly's head is on the chopping block again. Facing page, below: The boys engaged in one of Curly's favorite pastimes. Above: The Stooges have to fill in for some chorus girls in Rhythm and Weep (1946). It was one of the last film appearances that Curly would make.

SING A SONG OF SIX PANTS

Shemp

After Curly's death in 1952, Moe and Larry didn't know how to proceed. Columbia presented a lot of replacement possibilities, but the few who seemed at all right were unavailable. The young Buddy Hackett declined Moe and Larry's offer, feeling that he could never fill Curly's shoes. Finally, the obvious solution occurred to them: Shemp.

Shemp was a great comedian, a former Stooge *and* a Howard brother! Columbia balked at the idea, saying that Moe and Shemp looked too much alike, but Moe himself countered with a threat to walk out. Columbia gave in, and *Fright Night* was made with Shemp in 1946.

Shemp made 77 films with Larry and Moe after *Fright Night*, often ad-libbing some very clever lines. In *Fright Night*, Moe grabbed Shemp by the lapels of his pin-stripe suit, and Shemp shook him off, saying, 'Watch it, you're bending my stripes.' Shemp's performance with the Three Stooges has often been slandered by loyal Curly fans; no one could have possibly taken the place of the super Stooge. But seen in his own right, Shemp was an extremely funny man, a masterful character actor and a skillful physical comic.

The Howard family has a compendium of 'Shemp stories.' Shemp and his wife brought live lobsters home for dinner one night, and Shemp's parents stopped by, surprise guests. Shellfish is not kosher, so Shemp quickly hid the lobsters in the shower stall. All night long, everyone could hear the loud clicking of the lobsters' claws. Shemp insisted that the racket was created by huge mice.

One Passover, Sol was reading the service at the seder very slowly. Shemp, Moe, Curly and their two brothers were famished; it was after 9:00 pm and still they hadn't eaten yet. Sol got up to wash his hands, and Shemp jumped up and turned the pages of Sol's book. When Sol returned, he sat down and continued his reading, never realizing that he was in an advanced spot. Shemp got away with this several times, giving new meaning to the word 'Passover.'

All of the Stooges were aficionados of the ponies and the ring. Attending a fight with Shemp, in particular, was an event not soon forgotten, especially if you were seated right next to him. Shemp would come out of his seat fighting, jabbing and weaving, sometimes endangering nearby spectators with his elbows. Yelling encouragement to his

Previous page: *Shemp Howard performs two feats: rips a phone book in half and regains his Stoogehood.*
Above: *Shemp rejoins brother Moe and Larry Fine in the act he had left 13 years earlier.*

chosen fighter, ranting at the ump, Shemp often had more people watching him than were watching the fight. Shemp died on 23 November 1955, after spending the day at the race track and the fights. On the way home that night in a friend's car, telling jokes and laughing, Shemp suddenly dropped his head, and with a smile on his face, he died.

Larry and Moe Lose Their Shorts, and A Couple of Joes

After Shemp's death, Larry suggested that they fulfill their contract for four more movies as the Two Stooges. Moe was so disheartened that he actually passed this ludicrous idea along to Columbia. Moe was grieving the loss of his second brother in three years, as well as worrying about the future of his livelihood in show business.

The newest Stooge proved to be close at hand: Shemp's close friend, Joe Besser. Joe and Shemp had worked together on ***The Passing Show of 1932*** and the 1949 movie ***Africa Screams*** with Abbott & Costello. Joe had even had some stooge experience with Milton Berle on television, and bore some physical resemblance to Curly. He was already under contract to Columbia, so new contracts were drawn up for 1956. Meanwhile, the question remained of fulfilling the 1955 contract. For the four remaining movies, Moe and Larry actually pieced together old stock footage, and augmented this with scenes with Shemp's double, Joe Palma.

Joe Besser made a fine third Stooge, a sissified mama's boy who never grew up, skipping and grinning at Moe and Larry. Joe had a clause written into his contract stipulating that Moe couldn't hit him. This was somewhat of a disappointment to audiences, because though the Stooges' humor is much more than slapstick, fans do expect Moe to dole out some punishment.

Despite the decrease in beatings, Stooges and fans alike were as happy as pie. Then the rumors began to fly: the entire Shorts Department at Columbia Pictures was on Death Row. On 20 December 1957, the Stooges completed their last short, **Sappy Bullfighters**, and the Shorts Department was no more.

In the Stooges' 24 years at Columbia (the longest commitment of any team in Hollywood), they starred in 194 shorts and five feature-length films. They received an Academy Award nomination in 1934 for **Men In**

Below left: *Moe, Shemp and Larry blow their tops.*
At bottom: *Moe is caught in the crossfire between his old partner and his new one, Joe Besser, in Guns A-Poppin' (1957).*
Overleaf: *When the Stooges stand in as cake decorators for Christine McIntyre, they accidentally use chewing gum instead of marshmallows, with sticky results.*

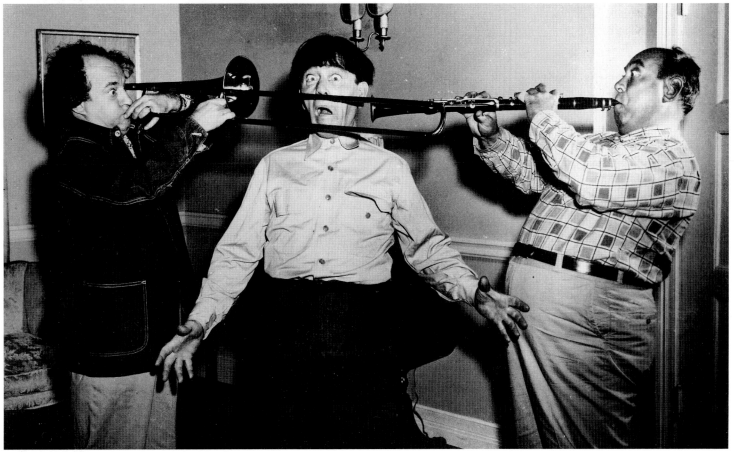

Above: *The Stooges join the space race when Curly-Joe DeRita joins the Stooges in* **Have Rocket Will Travel** *(1959).*
Facing page, above: *Larry has a hair-raising experience during the filming of* **Snow White and the Three Stooges** *(1961).*
Facing page, below: *Curly-Joe, Larry and Moe take on Sampson Burke in* **The Three Stooges Meet Hercules** *(1962).*

Black, and secured the Exhibitor's Laurel Awards so often that people began to refer to it as 'the Stooge award.' For five years running—1950 to 1954—their films were the top two-reel money-makers.

The Three Stooges Go Around the World in a Daze

Larry and Moe weren't quite ready to become retired guys yet. While in Las Vegas with his wife in 1958, Larry ran into his old friend Joe DeRita. In the 1920s, Joe had been playing the burlesque houses when the Stooges were on the vaudeville circuit. He and Larry had always enjoyed one another's company and stolen each other's jokes whenever their paths crossed. Now they agreed to work together—whenever Joe DeRita's schedule would allow it. They began with some stage appearances in California. Some went well. Some bombed beyond belief.

Just when the Stooges seemed completely washed up, Columbia released 78 old Stooges shorts to television as a marketing experiment. They were a smash hit, scoring the number one position in almost every after-school market in the country. The personal appearances began to sell out again across the country, wherever they had television.

The Stooges didn't receive a dime from their television reign, however; the Screen Actors' Guild didn't stipulate residuals for movies made before 1959, and Columbia had purchased the entire Stooge package, even for use on mediums *yet to be invented*. Indirectly, of course, the television exposure saved their careers from an early demise by generating new interest in the Stooges.

The Stooges were also suddenly the focus of enormous controversy, as well, concerning the violence of the shows. The general outcry was somewhat diffused by the efforts of television announcers such as Sally Starr, who broadcast out of Philadelphia. Sally provided her viewers with valuable lessons on distinguishing between *real* violence and the cartoonish violence of the Stooges.

Movie Maniacs

With their rediscovery in the late 1950s and early 1960s, the Stooges were suddenly receiving a great many movie offers from the new Hollywood. Their delight was mixed with bewilderment: 'In the old days, I didn't "take meetings," ' Larry said. 'I took beatings!'

Moe's son-in-law, Norman Maurer, took the helm of the ship of fools, wrote their scripts and eventually directed the trio in three of their feature films. Of Maurer's first effort, **The Stooges Meet Hercules**, the **New York Times** said in 1962, 'The picture is, of course, about as subtle as a bulldozer. But credit Moe, Larry and Curly-Joe with stepping on the gas. Hurry back, boys, and don't forget the pies.'

Their next effort that same year, **The Three Stooges In Orbit**, got an even better reception. The 11 July 1962 issue of *Variety* reported that the movie followed 'the classic pattern of "Stooges" comedy: three heads are better than one, if jarred together at periodic intervals.'

In 1965, Heritage Productions created an animated series called **The New Stooges**. The 156 episodes featured some live-action appearances by Larry, Joe DeRita and Moe.

The boys also loaned themselves out to other studios for brief appearances in films. As icons of buffoonery with worldwide recognition, all they had to do for some roles was show up. At the end of the movie **It's a Mad, Mad, Mad, Mad World**, almost all of the enormous cast ends up on a broken fire escape dangling many stories above the ground. Everyone waits breathlessly for the rescue squad to save the day. Larry, Moe and 'Curly-Joe' DeRita appear dressed as firemen. They are on screen for just a moment. Without their saying a word or doing a thing, everyone in the audience got the joke: with the Stooges to the rescue, the people on the fire escape were doomed.

In 1971, the boys decided to do a television movie called **Kooks' Tour**, a travel film in which the Stooges wreak havoc on the National Park System. Off across America in a caravan of campers went the Stooges, Norman Maurer (the producer-director), cameramen, technicians, and their co-star, a black Labrador named Moose. The entire film was ad-libbed.

In one scene shot in Yellowstone National Park, the Stooges become con artists. They produce a contraption of pipes and valves, and attempt to convince some tourists that they control the geysers. They check their watches, turn some valves and Old Faithful erupts for an amazed crowd. The rangers arrive on the scene in a cacophony of sirens, and the boys take it on the lam.

Later, some rangers expressed their disapproval of the scene, stating that the viewers would believe that the Stooges actually were controlling the geysers.

Unfortunately, very few viewers have ever had a chance to make that mistake. **Kooks' Tour** was never released. After the location shots were done and the crew returned to Los Angeles to do closeups, Larry suffered a stroke. He remained in the Motion Picture Country House & Hospital until his final stroke, on 9 January 1975.

Oil's Well That Ends Well

After Larry's first stroke, Moe decided that it was time to 'throw in the pies' and retire the Stooges. He signed up with an agent for character roles, but producers seemed hesitant, believing that the Stooge in him might show through, so he toured the lecture circuits, speaking mostly at colleges.

Moe used to pass cards out to the audience so he could conduct a question-and-answer session from the stage. One of the cards was returned with an unusual question on it: 'Would you throw a pie at me?'

Moe called the young man up on stage. He had come equipped with his own pie, but Moe explained that the pies *he* threw were whipped cream with cardboard backing. This pie had real crusts, a tin backing, and was full of heavy fruit. The young man would not be deterred, however, and Moe obliged. The young man was knocked back about five feet, but was extremely grateful. Moe got the standing ovation of his career.

He became a semi-regular on the Mike Douglas show, throwing pies in the faces of other celebrities such as Soupy Sales and Ted Knight. On one memorable visit, Helen, his wife of 49 years, got Dead-Shot himself with a sneaky pie-in-the-face.

Moe was busily taping and transcribing his memoirs at the time of his death in May 1975, bringing down the curtain on one of comedy's most popular teams.

Facing page, above: The Three Stooges Go Around the World in a Daze (1963) *and meet their triple doubles.*
Facing page, below: *Everyone's counting on the Stooges to save the day at the end of the movie,* **It's a Mad, Mad, Mad, Mad World** *(1963).*
These aliens think Curly-Joe, Larry and Moe should put their heads together in **The Three Stooges in Orbit** *(1962).*

IN THE SWEET PIE AND PIE

The Stooges have had a wide-ranging effect on popular culture: television, rock-and-roll, greeting cards, advertising and all kinds of merchandising.

In 1991, on David Letterman's list of the 'Top Ten Least Likely Things the CIA will Call Saddam Hussein,' number four was 'Stoogeophile.' In an episode of the television show **Cheers**, the lead character, Sam Malone, is worried that his whole life revolves around women. One of his friends, Norm Peterson, comforts him, 'Sam, you're a *Stooges fan*! Women hate the Stooges!'

On another television series, **Alien Nation**, a female alien and a male Earthling discuss the Stooges. The alien is not impressed. She finds their use of 'Nyuk, nyuk' to be offensive; the phrase is an obscenity in her language.

Not even academia is safe from these jesters: a French PhD candidate wrote a psychological treatise featuring the Stooges. He theorizes that each of the Stooges represents a stage of a man's development. Curly is, of course, the child, at the mercy of his environment. Larry is

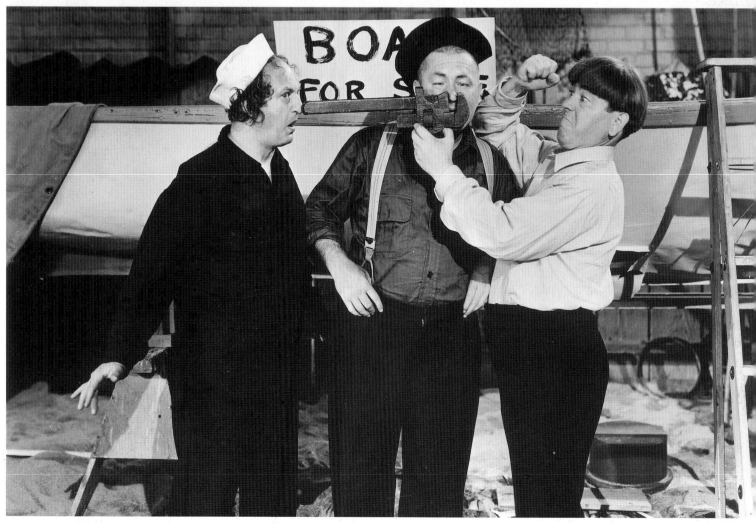

the young man, not knowing whether to side with Moe, the authority figure, or with defenseless Curly. Finally there's Moe, the older man, the leader, in control of everything but his temper, making the others quake.

The Stooges have also had an impact on popular music. James Jewel Osterberg took the appellation Iggy Stooge when he began his seminal punk band The Stooges, later changing his name to Iggy Pop. The story goes that he chose 'Stooges' because one band member had had a Moe-like bowl haircut when they were friends in high school. But the name proved appropriate for other reasons, as well. The rock-and-roll band possessed some expressly 'Three Stooges' characteristics: as the originals did with comedy, Iggy and his Stooges brought music to its glorious, no-frills lowest common denominator, its wildly illogical conclusion. Gusto snubbed its nose at sophistication.

The Three Stooges have been used to sell everything from children's cupcakes to US Savings Bonds to beer. Greeting cards carry the familiar likenesses, as well as the maxims of Stoogedom such as 'Why Soitenly!' and 'A Victim of Soicumstances.' Some bear clever Stooges jokes, such as this one: 'Have a Stooges kind of birthday. Eat, Drink and Beat Larry.'

Of course, the Stooges will cuff, whack, slap, *triple*-slap, yank, poke, kick and trip each other on into eternity, on celluloid and videotape, and in the minds of their many fans. *That's* the big idea, in answer to Larry's recurring question. Why, soitenly.

Page 74: *Curly and Moe go for a joy ride, with Larry trapped in the middle.*
Page 75: *Three decades later, Curly still plays the women's roles, like he did in the Howard family basement with Moe and Shemp. Here he is in* Time Out For Rhythm *(1941).*
Facing page, above: *The Stooges—and their popularity—skyrocketed in the late 1950s, around the time of the release of* Have Rocket, Will Travel.
Facing page, below: *Moe puts Larry and Curly's noses out of joint.*
Above: *Christine McIntyre leads the Stooges in a chorus line as they shuffle off to Buffalo.*

FILMOGRAPHY

Ted Healy and His Stooges
(Shemp, Moe and Larry)

Soup to Nuts (20th Century-Fox, 1930)
Turn Back the Clock (MGM, 1933)
Beer and Pretzels (MGM, 1933)
Hello Pop (MGM, 1933)
Meet the Baron (MGM, 1933)
Plane Nuts (MGM, 1933)
Dancing Lady (MGM, 1933)
Fugitive Lovers (MGM, 1934)
Hollywood Party (MGM, 1934)
The Big Idea (MGM, 1934)

The Three Stooges
(Larry, Curly and Moe)
All for Columbia Pictures

Women Haters (1934)
Punch Drunks (1934)
Men in Black (1934)
The Captain Hates the Sea (1934)
Three Little Pigskins (1934)
Horses' Collars (1935)
Restless Knights (1935)
Pop Goes the Easel (1935)
Uncivil Warriors (1935)
Pardon My Scotch (1935)
Hoi Polloi (1935)
Three Little Beers (1935)
Ants in the Pantry (1936)
Movie Maniacs (1936)
Half-Shot Shooters (1936)
Disorder in the Court (1936)
A Pain in the Pullman (1936)
False Alarms (1936)
Whoops I'm an Indian (1936)
Slippery Silks (1936)
Grips, Grunts, and Groans (1937)
Dizzy Doctors (1937)
Three Dumb Clucks (1937)
Back to the Woods (1937)
Goofs and Saddles (1937)
Cash and Carry (1937)
Playing the Ponies (1937)
The Sitter-Downers (1937)
Start Cheering (1937)
Termites of 1938 (1938)
Wee Wee Monsieur (1938)
Tassels in the Air (1938)
Flat Foot Stooges (1938)
Healthy, Wealthy, and Dumb (1938)

Violent is the Word for Curly (1938)
Three Missing Links (1938)
Mutts to You (1938)
Three Little Sew and Sews (1939)
We Want Our Mummy (1939)
A-Ducking They Did Go (1939)
Yes, We Have No Bonanza (1939)
Saved by the Belle (1939)
Calling All Curs (1939)
Oily to Bed, Oily to Rise (1939)
Three Sappy People (1939)
You Nazty Spy (1940)
Rockin' Through the Rockies (1940)
A-Plumbing We Will Go (1940)
Nutty But Nice (1940)
How High Is Up? (1940)
From Nurse to Worse (1940)
No Census, No Feeling (1940)
Cuckoo Cavaliers (1940)
Boobs in Arms (1940)
So Long, Mr Chumps (1941)
Dutiful But Dumb (1941)
All the World's a Stooge (1941)
I'll Never Heil Again (1941)
Time Out For Rhythm (1941)
An Ache in Every Stake (1941)
In the Sweet Pie and Pie (1941)
Some More of Samoa (1941)
Loco Boy Makes Good (1942)
Cactus Makes Perfect (1942)
What's the Matador? (1942)
Matri-Phony (1942)
Three Smart Saps (1942)
Even as IOU (1942)
My Sister Eileen (1942)
Sock-A-Bye Baby (1942)
They Stooge to Conga (1943)
Dizzy Detectives (1943)
Back From the Front (1943)
Spook Louder (1943)
Three Little Twerps (1943)
Higher Than a Kite (1943)
I Can Hardly Wait (1943)
Dizzy Pilots (1943)
Phony Express (1943)
A Gem of a Jam (1943)
Crash Goes the Hash (1944)
Busy Buddies (1944)
The Yoke's On Me (1944)
Idle Roomers (1944)
Gents Without Cents (1944)
No Dough, Boys (1944)

Three Pests in a Mess (1945)
Booby Dupes (1945)
Idiots Deluxe (1945)
Rockin' in the Rockies (1945)
If a Body Meets a Body (1945)
Micro-Phonies (1945)
Beer Barrel Polecats (1946)
Swing Parade of 1946 (1946)
   (feature for Monogram)
A Bird in the Head (1946)
Uncivil Warbirds (1946)
Three Troubledoers (1946)
Monkey Businessmen (1946)
Three Loan Wolves (1946)
GI Wanna Go Home (1946)
Rhythm and Weep (1946)
Three Little Pirates (1946)
Half-Wits' Holiday (1947)

The Three Stooges
(Larry, Shemp and Moe)

Fright Night (1947)
Out West (1947)
Hold That Lion (1947)
Brideless Groom (1947)
Sing a Song of Six Pants (1947)
All Gummed Up (1947)
Shivering Sherlocks (1948)
Pardon My Clutch (1948)
Squareheads of the Round Table (1948)
Fiddlers Three (1948)
Hot Scots (1948)
Heavenly Daze (1948)
I'm a Monkey's Uncle (1948)
Mummy's Dummies (1948)
Crime on Their Hands (1948)
The Ghost Talks (1949)
Who Done It? (1949)
Hocus Pocus (1949)
Fuelin' Around (1949)
Malice in the Palace (1949)
Vagabond Loafers (1949)
   (remake of **A-Plumbing We Will Go**)
Dunked in the Deep (1949)
Punchy Cowpunchers (1950)
Hugs and Mugs (1950)
Dopey Dicks (1950)
Love at First Bite (1950)
Self-Made Maids (1950)
Three Hams on Rye (1950)
Studio Stoops (1950)

Slap-Happy Sleuths (1950)
A Snitch in Time (1950)
Three Arabian Nuts (1951)
Baby Sitters' Jitters (1951)
Don't Throw That Knife (1951)
Scrambled Brains (1951)
Merry Mavericks (1951)
The Tooth Will Out (1951)
Gold Raiders (1951)
   (feature for United Artists)
Hula La La (1951)
The Pest Man Wins (1951)
   (remake of *Ants in the Pantry*)
A Missed Fortune (1952)
   (remake of *Healthy, Wealthy and Dumb*)
Listen, Judge (1952)
Corny Casanovas (1952)
He Cooked His Goose (1952)
Gents in a Jam (1952)
Three Dark Horses (1952)
Cuckoo on a Choo Choo (1952)
Up in Daisy's Penthouse (1953)
Booty and the Beast (1953)
Loose Loot (1953)
Tricky Dicks (1953)
Spooks (1953) (in 3-D)
Pardon My Backfire (1953)
Rip, Sew and Stitch (1953)
Bubble Trouble (1953)
Goof on the Roof (1953)
Income Tax Sappy (1954)
Musty Musketeers (1954)
Pals and Gals (1954)
Knutzy Knights (1954) (remake of
   Squareheads of the Round Table)
Shot in the Frontier (1954)
Scotched in Scotland (1954)
   (remake of *Hot Scots*)
Fling in the Ring (1955)
   (remake of *Fright Night*)
Of Cash and Hash (1955)
Gypped in the Penthouse (1955)
Bedlam in Paradise (1955)
Stone Age Romeos (1955)
   (remake of *I'm a Monkey's Uncle*)
Wham Bam Slam (1955)
Hot Ice (1955)
Blunder Boys (1955)
Husbands Beware (1956)

Creeps (1956)
Flagpole Jitters (1956)
   (remake of *Hocus Pocus*)
For Crimin' Out Loud (1956)
Rumpus in the Harem (1956)
Hot Stuff (1956)
Scheming Schemers (1956)
   (remake of *Vagabond Loafers* and
   A-Plumbing We Will Go)
Commotion on the Ocean (1956)

The Three Stooges
(Larry, Moe and Joe Besser)

Hoofs and Goofs (1957)
Muscle Up a Little Closer (1957)
A Merry Mix-up (1957)
Space Ship Sappy (1957)
Guns A-Poppin' (1957)
Horsing Around (1957)
Rusty Romeos (1957)
   (remake of *Corny Casanovas*)
Outer Space Jitters (1957)
Quiz Whiz (1958)
Fifi Blows Her Top (1958)
Pies and Guys (1958)
   (remake of *Half-Wits' Holiday*)
Flying Saucer Daffy (1958)
Oil's Well That Ends Well (1958)
   (remake of *Oily to Bed, Oily to Rise*)
Triple Crossed (1958)
   (remake of *He Cooked His Goose*)
Sappy Bullfighters (1958)
   (remake of *What's the Matador?*)

The Three Stooges
(Larry, Moe and Curly-Joe DeRita)

Have Rocket, Will Travel (1959) (feature)
Stop! Look! Laugh! (1960)
   (feature compilation of shorts)
Three Stooges Scrapbook (1960) (feature)
Snow White and the Three Stooges (1961)
   (20th Century-Fox feature)
The Three Stooges Meet Hercules (1962)
   (feature)
The Three Stooges in Orbit (1962) (feature)
*The Three Stooges Go Around the World
   in a Daze* (1963) (feature)

It's a Mad, Mad, Mad, Mad World (1963)
   (United Artists feature)
Four for Texas (1964) (Warner Bros feature)
The Outlaws Is Coming (1965) (feature)

Moe Howard

Space Master X-7 (1958)
   (feature for 20th Century-Fox)
Senior Prom (1959) Associate Producer
Don't Worry, We'll Think of a Title (1966)
   (feature for 20th Century-Fox)
Doctor Death, Seeker of Souls (1973)
   (feature for Cinerama)

Shemp Howard
As Knobby Walsh in the Joe Palooka shorts
   (Vitaphone, 1934-37)

Headin' East (1938)
Hollywood Roundup (1938)
Millionaires in Prison (1940)
The Leather Pushers (1940)
Give Us Wings (1940)
The Bank Dick (1940)
Meet the Chump (1941)
Buck Privates (1941)
The Invisible Woman (1941)
Six Lessons From Madame La Zonga (1941)
Mr Dynamite (1941)
In the Navy (1941)
Tight Shoes (1941)
San Antonio Rose (1941)
Hold That Ghost (1941)
Hit the Road (1941)
Too Many Blondes (1941)
Hellzapoppin' (1941)
The Strange Case of Dr Rx (1942)
Butch Minds the Baby (1942)
Mississippi Gambler (1942)
Private Buckaroo (1942)
Pittsburgh (1942)
Arabian Nights (1942)
Keep 'em Slugging (1943)
It Ain't Hay (1943)
How's About It? (1943)
Strictly in the Groove (1943)
Crazy House (1943)
Moonlight and Cactus (1944)
Strange Affair (1944)
Three of a Kind (1944)
Blondie Knows Best (1946)
Dangerous Business (1946)
The Gentleman Misbehaves (1946)
One Exciting Week (1946)
Africa Screams (1949)

Joe Besser

Hot Steel (1940)
Africa Screams (1949)
Woman In Hiding (1950)
The Desert Hawk (1950)
Say One For Me (1959)
Let's Make Love (1960)

Joe DeRita

The Doughgirls (1944)
The Bravados (1958)

INDEX